Think Better Workbook

A hands-on, practical companion to the breakthrough book
Make the Leap: Think Better, Train Better, Run Faster.

By Bryan Green

Make the Leap "Think Better Workbook"

Cover Artwork by Nadine Denten (@nadineinjapan)

maketheleapbook.com
maketheleapbook@gmail.com
@maketheleapbook

Praise for *Make the Leap*

"If *Make the Leap* had been available I would have strongly encouraged the athletes I've coached over the years to read it at the start of each season. Furthermore I would have suggested that they review the book whenever they ran into mental or physical blocks."
- Bob Larsen, 4xNCAA Coach of the Year, UCLA, Retired; 2004 US Olympic Distance Coach; Head Toad

"Bryan Green was a great teammate to me at UCLA. He is a student of the sport of both on and off the track. His education, experiences, observations, and insights will help get you to the next level. I highly recommend his book, *Make the Leap*."
- Meb Keflezighi, Olympic marathon silver medalist, Boston and New York City Marathon champion

"*Make the Leap* will transform how you think about your training, which in turn will transform your entire running experience. If you feel you have untapped potential, read this book."
- Matt Fitzgerald, Author of *80/20 Running* and *Chasing the Dream*

"The next leap forward in achieving higher levels of peak performance will come from understanding our mental relationship with running. *Make the Leap* provides an easy to use framework for improving your mental skills, honing a growth mindset, and achieving your potential."
- Jason Fitzgerald, Strength Running head coach and host of the Strength Running Podcast

"*Make the Leap* is a *legal* performance-enhancing aid for athletes and coaches alike. It is truly a cheat code and hack on the odyssey of becoming a champion. When you read this book, make sure you do so with a highlighter and pen in hand because there are non-stop "a-ha" moments. Green deftly applies time-tested social psychological principles to sport performance in a very relatable and easy-to-understand way that results in the first singular, "must-have" resource for the bookshelves of all endurance athletes and coaches."
- Scott Abbott, Executive Director, Sacramento Running Association; former coach at Sacramento State University

"I witnessed Bryan Green make the leap when we were teammates at UCLA. His level of confidence in every practice and every race that season left an impression on me that inspired my ascension to the top of our sport. Take it from me, he knows what it takes to break free of the mental barriers that prevent us from realizing our full potential. *Make the Leap* will show you the way."
- Jon Rankin, 3:52 miler, US Olympic 1500m alternate; Founder, Go Be More Apparel

"*Make the Leap* will help runners prioritize what's important in their training. But this is not just a book for runners—it can help anyone on their athletic journey, or any mental or physical health odyssey."
- Christian Cushing-murray, 3:55 miler, Masters M45 1500m record holder, Century High track coach

"It is so good to have a book that looks into the mindset of the athlete and analyses the critical questions of how to think about training to get the best out of yourself. Bryan Green accepts the 'how' and 'when' but provides the definitive 'why' that separates the best from the rest. I encourage you to 'make the leap', you won't regret it."
- Steve Moneghetti, Olympian, Commonwealth Games Marathon Champion

See more at maketheleapbook.com/praise

Think Better Workbook

First and foremost: thank you for investing in this workbook, and in your success!

This workbook is a companion to my book *Make the Leap: Think Better, Train Better, Run Faster*. For those who've read it, this workbook provides a hands-on tool to help you apply everything we learned. For those who haven't, no worries! It was made to exist independently. So while it lacks many of the stories, data, diagrams, and detailed explanations you get in the book, I'm confident you will still get 80/20 value from it (I explain what 80/20 means on page 17).

Make the Leap is centered around one key idea: **Think better, train better.** What most athletes lack is a mental framework for thinking about their training. *Make the Leap* provides this framework in the form of 11 Optimal Training Principles and 4 mental model Spotlights. This workbook includes a one-page summary of each chapter and spotlight, with tactical questions to help you turn the concepts into Next Step goals you can build into your training today.

I made this workbook to serve a few key groups:

Coaches
Whether or not you ask your athletes to read the book, it's critical that you talk about these topics. If all of your athletes have this workbook, it will allow you to systematically build these concepts into your program. And if your athletes can't get the workbook individually, I've designed it to be easy to print, one chapter summary at a time!

Athletes
I know you want to get the most out of your training. And I'm sure you gained tons of ideas from the book. But it's critical that you think about and write down exactly what you plan to do to get better. This workbook will help you engage better, take more responsibility, and make your new Systems, Next Step goals, and Purposeful Practice strategies concrete.

Parents
It's tough to connect with your kids about what they are going through. It's critical that you adopt a shared language and framework, or else you'll simply talk right past each other. Whether you've read the book or just the workbook, this will ensure you both have enough of an understanding to have productive conversations about each of the key principles.

Regardless of your experience or role in training, this workbook will give you the tools to think better, train better, and then...Make the Leap!

Go Be More,
Bryan

The Optimal Training Principles

1. Your athletic performance is a result of your attitude, your effort, and your training methods.

2. Active engagement in training makes the process more understandable, more relevant, and more effective. (And more fun.)

3. You are responsible for your own training.

4. Ability is a variable, not a constant. The harder you work, the more able you become.

5. Self-efficacy is a fundamental ingredient to overcoming obstacles and achieving success.

6. All behavior is caused. All causation is mental. We become what we think about most of the time.

7. Optimal training is centered on clear, executable goals. We train to improve specific abilities.

8. Certain behaviors, if practiced with consistent quality, ensure Optimal Training.

9. Making mistakes is an effective way to learn and improve.

10. Racing times and personal records indicate progress at one point in time.

11. Optimal performances and realizing your potential are results of painstaking preparation and hard work.

The Four Spotlights

1. The Momentum Model - a simple tool to understand what's driving you forward, and what's holding you back

2. Attribution Theory - what we say defines how we think; and high achievers speak differently from low achievers

3. The 80/20 Rule - not all behaviors drive the same results; when we identify what really matters we get much more out of our time and effort

4. Next Level 80/20 - when we get serious about applying the 80/20 rule, we see that most of our progress comes from just a few activities

But first...what is "a leap" anyway?

Chapter 1: What is a Leap?

We typically think of improvement as linear, but in fact it is a process of slow growth punctuated with minor spurts of rapid improvement we call leaps. **Leaps are the normal process of improvement when you are training correctly!**

The biggest leap I know of was made by my teammate Jon Rankin. He went from a very good 3:47 1500m runner to a world class 3:35 1500m runner in one season. While most of us do not experience leaps of that magnitude, the shape of the improvement when we plot in on a chart looks roughly the same (Fig 1).

Anyone can make a leap in their performance. You probably already have, and you will again, assuming you are training the right way. A leap is the natural output of maintaining a positive feedback loop in your training. That feedback loop looks like Figure 3.

When your feedback loop is creating positive change, and that change is consistently being fed back into your training, you create the condition for a leap. Leaps are the result of consistent, high quality feedback loops.

(Sidenote: there is actual math that explains this. It's called compounding. When each cycle improves on your previous improvement, you get a curve like the one below.)

A "leap cycle" has three main stages: **Build, Leap, and Sustain**. The Build phase doesn't indicate any major improvement is happening, but it is laying the foundation. The Leap phase is when the compounding kicks in and you improve rapidly. The Sustain phase is when you plateau having reached your short-term potential (Fig 8).

The size of the leap is determined by the quality and consistency of your feedback loop. If you make a positive change to your training after making a leap–either quality or quantity–you will enter a new Build phase and create the condition for another leap.

This process can be repeated indefinitely until you reach your potential. But remember! All leaps are preceded by a positive change in your training. If your quality doesn't improve after making a leap, you will not make another one.

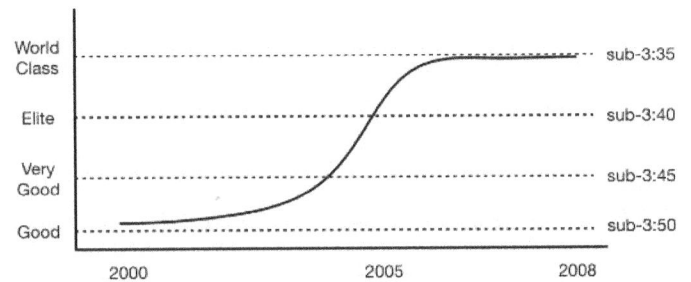

Fig 1 - Jon Rankin's leap charted on a graph

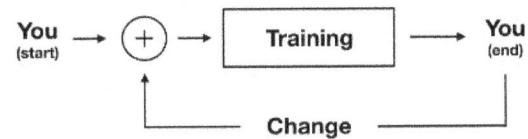

Fig 3 - In a training program, training is the process and the feedback is your improvement at the end of the training period

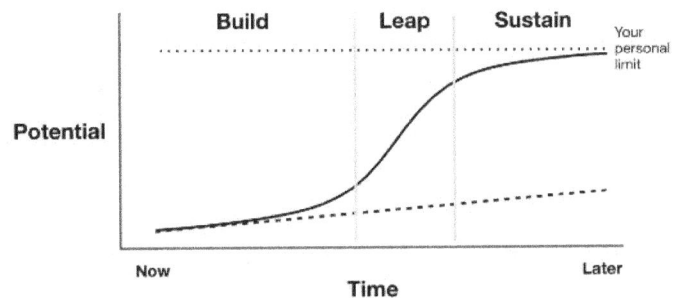

Fig 8 - Our Leap Cycle consists of 3 phases: Build, Leap, Sustain.

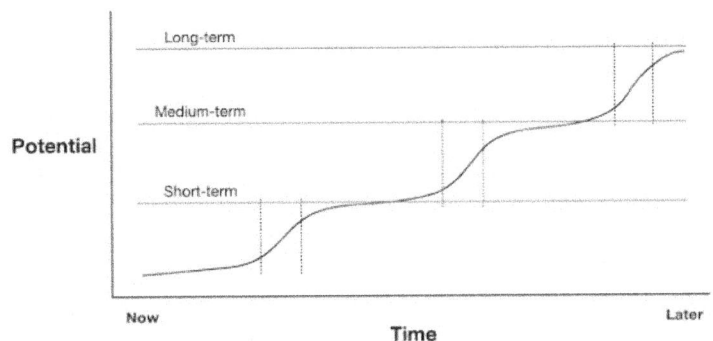

Fig 9 - Reaching our long-term potential requires us to continually create new leap cycles

Build It In

1. Think of some things you're good at. It can be school, sports, hobbies, anything. Did you ever find it was suddenly easier than before? That it just clicked? I bet it's happened many times. Those were leaps! Write down a couple examples here.

2. Quality and consistency lead to a leap. What are one or two areas of your training where you can definitely improve your quality?

3. What are one or two areas--in practice or outside of practice--that you can improve your consistency?

4. How can you ensure your improvement from today gets carried over to tomorrow? Write down a few ideas and discuss them with your coach.

Spotlight: The Momentum Model

Imagine you are a ball. You are on an uphill path with a goal at the end. The height of the goal is the amount you have to improve to achieve it. The length of the path is how long it will take to get there (Fig 10).

To reach your goal, you have to pick up enough momentum (i.e., improve) to ascend the hill and overcome any potential obstacles on the path. Where your ball sits represents your current ability. From your current position there are three possibilities: go forward, go backward, or stay where you are.

Now imagine that there are **positive forces** that make you roll faster, and **negative forces** that slow you down. Simple, right? The more the positive forces outweigh the negative, the faster you will roll toward your goal.

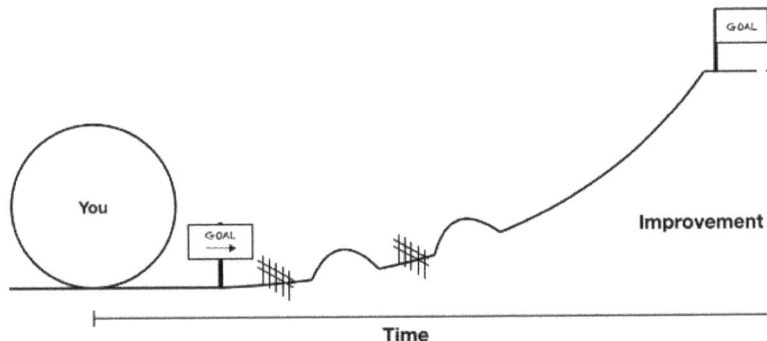

Fig 10 - To achieve a goal, you need to generate sufficient momentum to climb the hill and overcome the obstacles in the way.

We can represent the positive and negative forces within you or outside you as arrows, with positive arrows pointing toward your goal and negative arrows pointing away (Fig 11). The only way to reach your goal is to get more or stronger arrows pointing in the right direction. You can A) increase the positive forces in your life, B) decrease the negative forces, or C) do both!

Internal forces fall into three categories: our health, our attitudes, and our efforts. **External forces** include the people and organizations in our lives, as well as our general environment. Some of these forces we control, others less so. Some of these push us forward and help us achieve our goals. Others hold us back. Some affect us personally, while others affect everyone. It is up to us to eliminate the negative forces or boost the positive ones.

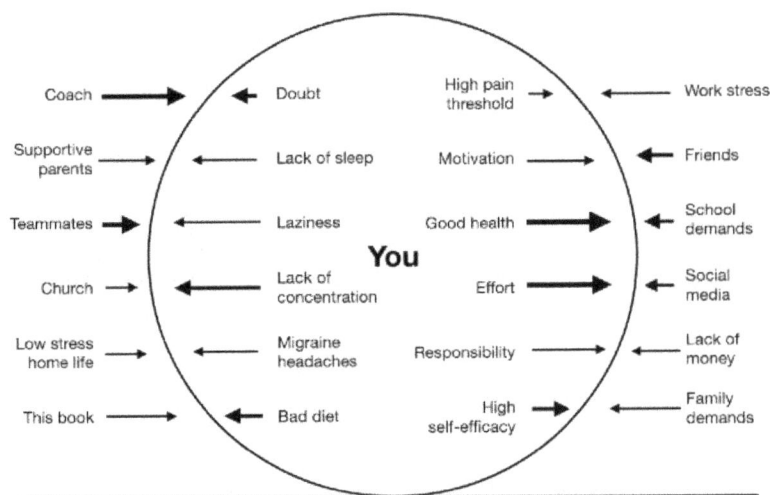

Fig 11 - The forces that move our ball can be positive or negative and internal or external.

You will face three kinds of obstacles. **Persistence obstacles** are things we can only overcome by digging in and pushing through them. **Preparation obstacles** are events that we can anticipate and strategize for. **Bad luck obstacles** are events we can't really prepare for. Obstacles rarely stop our progress, but they often slow us down. The best way to overcome an obstacle is to anticipate it and avoid it. If that's not possible, it is best to have a system to maintain as much positive momentum as possible when you hit them.

Build It In:

1. Fill out your own Momentum Model. Add any forces that you feel are affecting your momentum. Draw the arrows bigger if the force is stronger.

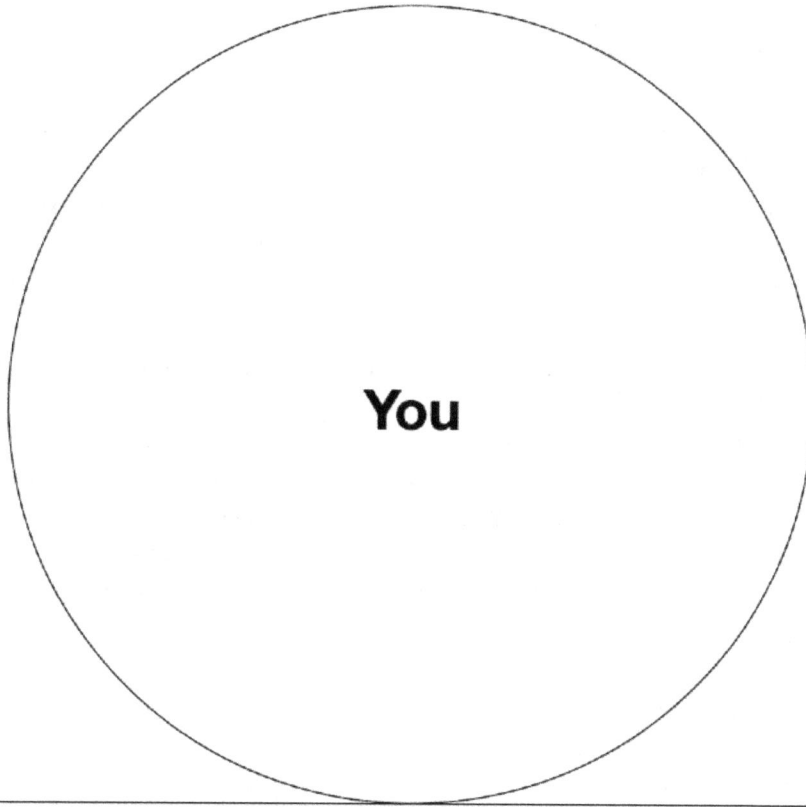

You

2. Bigger forces are generally more important than smaller ones. Look at the big ones. Which do you want to improve right now?

3. What are a few obstacles you need to watch out for? Are they persistence, preparation, or bad luck obstacles?

Chapter 2: Optimal Training Pyramid

Training is only as complicated as you choose to make it, and the same goes for your mental approach.

Optimal Training Principle (OTP) #1: Your athletic performance is a result of your attitude, effort, and training methods. Attitude forms the foundation of your success... or your failure. Your effort is dependent on your attitude. Your effort also affects the quality of your training methods. Your training affects your results (Fig 13).

We all have different personalities, but there are a few key attitudes all great performers share. Having a belief in the power of hard work is most important. Success is never solely due to hard work, but effort is the one variable you can control. Other essential attitudes include high engagement, responsibility, discipline, and pride.

Fig 13 - The Optimal Training Pyramid - Attitude is the foundation. Effort is based on it, and Training Methods refine it.

The simplest way to analyze effort is to break it down into its three main components: quality, quantity, and time. You can do something better, do more of it, or do it longer. ***Start by focusing on quality***, because quality is harder to maintain the more you increase quantity and time.

There is a direct connection between how you think about your training and the quality of your effort. As your attitude improves, so does your quality. As your mental approach becomes consistently great, your workouts will become consistently high quality. Champions live in this range (Fig 14).

Quality is determined by the workout's purpose. It is a measure of execution, and execution is about how well your actions align with your purpose. Don't increase quantity at the expense of quality. Strive to have 100% quality in whatever you're doing. It's better to execute an imperfect workout to the best of your abilities than to do a perfect workout poorly. If you maximize your quality over a sustained period of time, you're doing enough to make a leap.

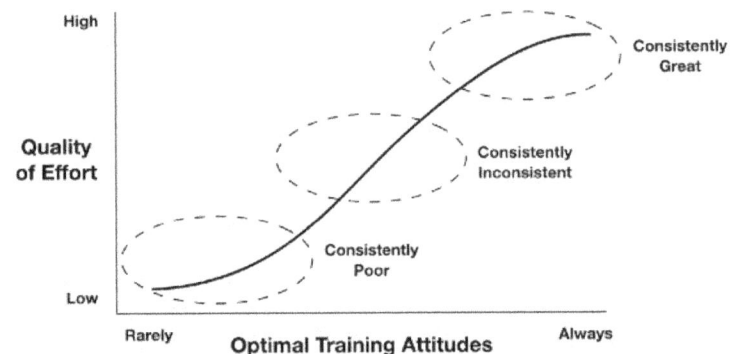

Fig 14 - The Attitude-Effort Curve. The more consistently your attitude is great, the higher quality your effort will be.

Our Training Methods are how we polish our 'raw materials'–our attitude, effort, and talent–into a finished product. Some are formal (i.e. your training sessions) and others are informal (i.e. your activities outside of practice). Each of these activities contributes to our overall performance.

Don't stress your training methods in the beginning. Focus instead on improving your mental approach, your preparation, and your effort. Regardless of how good your workouts are, this will ensure you get the most out of them.

Build It In:

1. Attitude is the foundation of your training. Do you consider yourself to have a strong mental approach to training? What is your biggest mental strength?

2. What is your biggest mental weakness?

3. Why is it better to get 100% out of a good workout than to get 70% out of a perfect workout?

4. How often do you get 100% out of your workouts? What simple changes can you make to help you do it?

5. **Systemize it:** Keep A Journal. Don't just track the basics, like mileage and splits and how your legs feel. Write down your feelings, too. Are you tired, stressed or distracted? Are you inspired, excited, or motivated? Training is about more than just running. Use the journal to help you identify forces that can be holding you back.

Chapter 3: Engagement

OTP #2: Active engagement in training makes the process more understandable, more relevant, and more effective (and more fun). Engagement is a critical attitude for success. It is what happens when *passion meets motivation* (Fig 16). Intelligence plus engagement leads to breakthroughs. Caring plus engagement leads to improvement. Curiosity plus engagement leads to learning. ***You need to be engaged.***

One sign of engagement is intense curiosity. The engaged athlete wants to know everything. Why am I doing these workouts? What are other people doing? How does this fit in the bigger picture? They ask good questions and explore other sources of information. The more they do, the more they understand themselves, their strengths and weaknesses, and their areas for improvement. One great way to engage: investigate when your results don't align with your expectations.

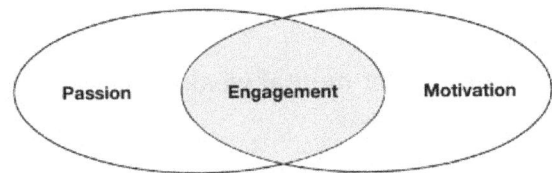

Fig 16 - Engagement is the result of passion meeting motivation.

Better understanding leads to a sense of perspective. This perspective improves your ability to make good decisions. It can't guarantee you will get the outcome you want, but it will help you make your decisions for the right reasons. Having a well-rounded perspective also helps you set better Next Step goals and manage your expectations throughout the season.

Better perspective leads to better actions in all areas of your life. There are two training programs that every athlete must carry out: the formal training program and the hidden training program.

- **Formal training program:** the official, formal, coach-approved program
- **Hidden training program:** everything you *really* need to do to be successful

The hidden training program includes everything you do outside practice, how you think about your training, and how you organize your life (Fig 17).

Here's a bonus: getting more engaged actually *makes training more fun.* Even something miserable like an ice bath can be made better. And the more you do this, the more you keep your momentum positive.

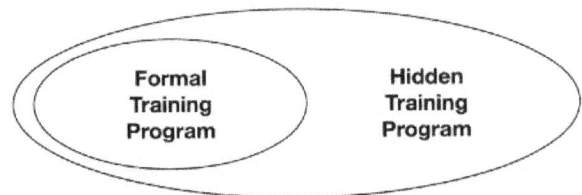

Fig 17 - The Hidden Training Program is everything you REALLY need to do to be successful. The Formal Training Program makes up just a part of it.

You have to be ready to work hard when you show up! Great athletes use their engagement to master the hidden training program, which sets them up for success in their formal training program.

Build It In:

1. On a scale of 1-5 (5 = high), how motivated are you to be the best runner you can be?

2. On a scale of 1-5, how passionate are you about running?

3. Think about your typical day. Does your engagement level align to the motivation and passion scores you just gave yourself? Is something holding you back?

4. **Get curious:** Why do you warm up the way you do? Why do you do the stretches you do? Why do you eat when you do? How much sleep do you need? The more you learn, the more tightly the pieces of the puzzle fit together.

5. Write down three lifestyle habits you have that could be holding you back. Why do you think you adopted these habits? How hard would it be to improve them?

6. **Systemize it:** Read a book about running. (Any book is fine, even fiction.) Don't just read it for fun. Read it purposefully.
   - Find three useful ideas you can build into your training.
   - Find three surprising facts you didn't know before.
   - Write them here and talk about them with your teammates or coach.

Chapter 4: Responsibility

OTP #3: You are responsible for your own training. Just as your coach's job is to get the best out of you, *your job is to get the most out of your coach*. Coach-Runner relationships where the athlete only takes responsibility for executing the workout aren't optimal. You need to take responsibility for all of your training. You aren't giving up your responsibility for planning and evaluation to your coach; you are delegating it because that is a coach's area of expertise.

Responsibility for Training: There are three main areas of your training where you will depend on your coach: Planning, Execution, and Evaluation.

You will always own the responsibility for your execution. You need to know what to do and then do it. When it comes to planning and evaluation, you should share this responsibility with your coach. In both cases, it is *your* responsibility to communicate openly and honestly about how you feel because that will affect the quality of your execution (Fig 20).

Responsibility for the Rest: Outside of formal practice, you need to take even more responsibility. In the Hidden Training Program you have to navigate all the other activities that can make or break your success. If you aren't sure how to do it, get help from your coach! They won't be able to do it for you, but they can certainly help you navigate the challenge (Fig 21).

Responsibility for Results means looking first to yourself when you don't perform as expected, not blaming workouts or external forces. Remember my tempo run story. I was so frustrated when my improvement plateaued and I entered a Sustain phase. I assumed something was wrong. I blamed one workout and allowed it to create doubt about my progress. When you think linearly, a leap can mess up all of your expectations (Fig 22).

Fundamentally, this also means taking responsibility for your expectations and making sure the planning leads to good results. Start with your execution and add in more as you go.

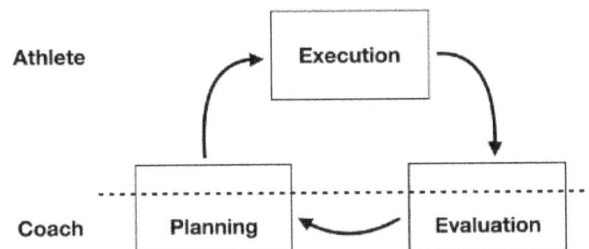

Fig 20 - The Optimal Division of Responsibility: the athletes shares some responsibility for planning and evaluation, too

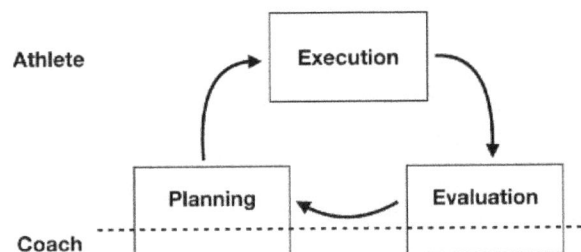

Fig 21 - Responsibility for the Hidden Training Program rests primarily with the athlete

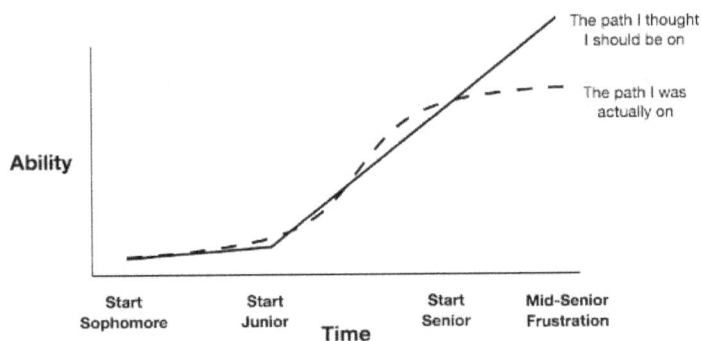

Fig 22 - Making a leap does not fit with linear expectations, and can cause frustrations when you come out of the Leap Phase and enter the Sustain Phase

Build It In:

1. Words we say can have up to 10x more impact on us than words we think.
When you get up in the morning, look in the mirror and say out loud, "I am responsible for today's results."
Hear yourself say it. Does saying it change how you feel?

2. How are you taking responsibility for Planning today? What can you do better?

3. How are you taking responsibility for Execution today? What can you do better?

4. How are you taking responsibility for Evaluation today? What can you do better?

5. **Systemize it:** Next time something doesn't work, stop and examine your role as honestly as you can. Did you set good expectations? Did you communicate well? Did you execute to your standards? Did you understand what was required? Figure out what you can do better.

Spotlight: Attribution Theory

Attribution is how we explain why things happen. For every event we create an explanation, a story we tell ourselves. Within those stories we attribute causes--correctly and incorrectly--to four factors (Fig 23):

- **Talent**: qualities inherent to who we are
- **Effort**: how hard we work
- **Task Difficulty**: how hard it is to do something
- **Luck**: things we couldn't reasonably expect, both good and bad.

The stories we tell and the language we use to tell them are learned. We pick it up from our parents, friends, TV, movies, music, and other social interactions. The more you hear something, the more likely you are to believe it. The more you believe it, the more likely you are to act on it.

There are three causal dimensions of an attribution (Fig 24).

- **Locus of Control**: internal (inside us) or external (within the outside world)
- **Stability**: variable (it changes) or fixed (it never changes)
- **Controllability:** can we control it?

To be controllable, a factor has to be both variable and internal. Effort is therefore the only controllable factor.

High Achievers internalize success. They attribute success to talent and effort. When they fail, however, they attribute it to variable factors, like how hard they work and bad luck. With high achievers, effort plays a key role in all performances.

Low achievers tend to externalize success, attributing it to the task being easy or having good luck. (Remember the math student I tutored?!). Even worse, low achievers tend to internalize failure, by attributing it to lack of talent and the task being too hard. Effort is rarely the focus of a low achiever (Fig 25).

Attribution can become a habit. Create a strong attribution habit by following Green's Razor: *Never attribute to talent or luck that which is adequately explained by effort.*

	Talent			**Effort**	
potential	natural	genius	train	slack off	procrastinate
knack	inherent weakness	strength	try	careless energy	idle work hard
	endowed	savant	give all we've got	struggle	toil
born to...	a head for...		prepare sluggish		endeavor
	gift comes easily	aptitude	give our best shot	lackadaisical	push
incompetent	capacity		exercise		
impotent	the right stuff*	savvy		put some elbow grease on it*	

	Task Difficulty			**Luck**	
tough		challenging	blessing		fate
impossible	difficult painful	hellish hard	fluke destiny		in the cards
crazy	demanding	basic a picnic	karma serendipity	fortune	a big/lucky break
complicated	obvious	a piece of cake	misfortune a raw deal		a perfect storm
simple	smooth a snap	straightforward	cursed a tough/bad break		jinxed
easy as ABC*	easy peasy lemon squeezy*		untimely	star-crossed	schlimazel*
				schlemiel*	

*grandparents only

Fig 23 - We use different words and phrases to attribute our success or failure to the four main factors

		Stability	
		Fixed	Variable
Locus of Control	Internal	Talent	Effort
	External	Task Difficulty	Luck

Controllable

Fig 24 - Each factor can be categorized by Stability, Locus of Control, and Controllability

		Attribution	
		Success	Failure
Athlete	High Achiever	• Talented • Worked hard	• Didn't work hard • Underestimated task • Bad luck
	Low Achiever	• Task was easy • Lucky	• Not talented • Task too difficult

Fig 25 - High achievers internalize success and treat failure as variable. Low achievers do the opposite.

Build It In:

1. Which of the four factors--talent, effort, task difficulty, and luck--do you think contributes the most to your success? How about your failure? Why?

2. Using the table above, which words or phrases do you catch yourself using a lot? (It's ok to use all of them, but effort-based terms should make up a large percentage of your attribution.)

3. When you see someone else succeed or fail, what is your default attribution? How do you explain it?

4. Do you attribute your success or failure in running to the same factors as school, or relationships, or video games? Why or why not? What's different about them?

5. **Systemize It:** When you hear other people attribute performance to talent or luck, convert it to effort-based terms in your head. The more you do this, the more natural it will become for you to think this way about *your* performances.

Chapter 5: Growth Mindset

OTP #4: Ability is a variable, not a constant. The harder you work, the more able you become. When we talk about elite athletes in terms of talent, we discredit the real difference between them and us: they have worked smarter and harder than us over a longer time period. Why did Meb win the Boston Marathon? His coach believes it's because "No athlete in history has probably done more drills than Meb." We see the victory. We don't see the 20 years of daily form drills.

There are two distinct ways of measuring "excellence." **Norm-referenced excellence** is success judged by external benchmarks, like time or place. It's also how others typically judge us (Fig 28).

Self-referenced excellence is success judged by inner standards of performance, like improvement and fulfillment. Great performers cultivate a focus on self-referenced excellence, and use norm-referenced measures as motivators and benchmarks.

	Type of Result	
Time Period	Norm-Referenced	Self-Referenced
Short-term	Fast Time Winner of Race	Improvement Optimal Performance
Long-term	Champion All-Time List Hall of Fame	Fulfillment Realize Potential

Fig 28 - Norm-referenced typically focuses on comparing, whereas self-referenced focuses on context

Focusing on self-referenced excellence has many benefits. It forces you to think about context instead of comparisons. It creates opportunities for learning and improvement: to try new things, test yourself, and fail with purpose. Even better, self-referenced achievements are often transferable to other areas of your life.

People typically fall into two distinct "mindsets" when they think about ability. A **Fixed mindset** thinks that our potential is limited and we can only hope to demonstrate our talents. A **Growth mindset** thinks that we can continue to learn and develop and that challenges are an opportunity to improve. A Fixed mindset leads to a desire to be great but a fear of failure. A Growth mindset leads to passion for whatever you dedicate yourself to and actual greatness (Fig 29).

	Qualities		
Mindset	Focus	Performance	Cultivates
Fixed	Norm-Referenced Achievement	Indication of Relative Position	Desire to Be Great
Growth	Self-Referenced Achievement	Indication of Progress	Actual Greatness

Fig 29 - Norm-referenced focus leads to a desire to be great; self-referenced leads to actual greatness

A Fixed mindset can be fixed (ahem, improved). There are two good methods. The **Reframing Approach** requires that you describe all results in effort and preparation-based terms. Take talent and luck out of the equation. The **Analogy Approach** involves showing someone how a field they think is talent-based–remember Betty Edwards's art classes–is actually effort and training-based. When you do this, it will help you to view other areas as potentially the same.

Build It In:

1. Write down a few of your bigger goals. How many of them are norm-referenced?

2. Do you respond differently to norm-referenced and self-referenced goals? How so?

3. Are there any areas in your life where you may have a fixed mindset? Write them down. (Many people have at least a couple.)

4. A fixed mindset is often a defense mechanism. More often than not, it stops us from doing the work we need to do to realize it's not true! Look at those examples above. Have you ever truly dedicated yourself to being great in those areas? Have you ever had top level coaching? What would happen if you did?

5. **Reframe It:** Think of someone successful whom everyone agrees is uber-talented. Now, research a little about how they trained. Retell the story of their success through the lens of effort, preparation, and training.

Now, ask yourself: are you working as hard as they did?

Chapter 6: Self-Efficacy

OTP #5: Self-efficacy is a fundamental ingredient to overcoming obstacles and achieving success. To make a leap, we need to maintain enough motivation to overcome the negative forces and obstacles in our way. Believing your effort will determine your outcomes for a specific task is essential to achieve big goals. Without it, you won't try in the first place.

Self-efficacy is not the same as self-esteem. Self esteem is how you feel about yourself. Self-efficacy focuses on potential outcomes; *it is what you believe you can accomplish given the effort you put into an activity.* Self-efficacy is an attitude, a way we view the world, and high self-efficacy leads to greatness (Fig 30).

	Measure of	Focus on	Valuable for
Self-Esteem	Self-worth	Feelings	Feeling good about yourself
Self-Efficacy	Ability to succeed	Outcomes	Accomplishing difficult tasks

Fig 30 - Self-esteem focuses on how you feel; self-efficacy focus on what you can achieve

There are four (plus two) types of experience that contribute to our self-efficacy (Fig 31):

Personal Experience is the most important. If you've done something once, you will believe you can do it again. It doesn't take much; it could be feeling great at the end of a hard workout, or staying close to a better runner longer than usual. In my case, it involved experiencing how much pain I could put myself through, which set a benchmark for every race after that.

Vicarious Experience is the second best way. This is seeing *someone you relate to* accomplish something. 'If he can do it, I can, too.' We often underestimate how powerful and important this is.

Social Persuasion—someone you trust saying you can do something—can also be effective, especially for those with little experience.

Physiological factors are how you feel in a situation. When you feel good, it boosts your self-efficacy. Train yourself for how it will feel and your efficacy will improve.

		Type of Factor	
		Internal	External
Effect on Self-Efficacy	High	Personal Experience	Vicarious Experience
	Low	Physiological; Visualization; Faith	Social Persuasion

Fig 31 - The 4(+2) ways of increasing self-efficacy. Personal experience is the strongest boost, followed by Vicarious experience

Though not part of standard self-efficacy theory, **visualization** and **faith** can also contribute to your high self-efficacy. Visualization creates a feeling that you've done it before, whereas faith ties your effort and performance to a higher purpose.

Lastly, one of the best ways to build self-efficacy is to persist in the face of adversity. Persistence and self-efficacy are their own feedback loop. The longer you persist, the more you believe you can. The more you believe you can, the longer you will persist. The longer you persist *with a positive feedback loop*, the more likely you are to make a leap.

Build It In:

1. **Personal Experience:** Think about your most recent personal best. How confident were you that you could do it when you first started running (possibly years before)? How confident were you one month prior to doing it? How about the day before? Our experience greatly affects our belief.

2. One more question: the day after your personal best, having done it once, how confident were you that you could do it again?

3. **Vicarious Experience:** Is there someone out there who has achieved your goal who seems like they are just like you? It can be a sibling, teammate, a rival, or whoever you identify with. Write down their names.

Now make this a mantra: If _____ can do it, I can, too!

4. **Personal+Vicarious Experience:** Think of times outside running when you were successful not because you were already good at something, but because you worked hard on it. It could be learning math concepts, a musical instrument, or beating a video game. Write it down.

When you're stuck, repeat this: I did it in _____, I can do it in this, too!

5. **Social Persuasion:** When you need a boost, ask your coach if they believe you can accomplish your goals. When they say yes, believe them! They know what they are talking about.

What are your goals? What did your coach say?

Spotlight: The 80/20 Rule

Yogi Berra once said: "Baseball is 90% mental. The other half is physical." He's right!

The 80/20 rule summarizes the idea that many relationships are disproportional, with 20% of one factor causing 80% of the other. (For example: 20% of people own 80% of property, or 20% of dishes generate 80% of restaurant revenues.)

When we visualize this we see that cause and effect are related but distinct, that a small number of activities generate the majority of our results, and that a large number of our activities generate a small portion of our results. *What we do and the results we receive are not proportional* (Fig 32).

The key question for each activity is, "How should I get the most out of this?" For **top 20%** activities, you should aim to get as much as possible--*to max them out*. For the **rest of 80%** activities, you want to do the minimum necessary. Your strategy should be to keep them as positive as possible *without putting any extra effort into them*. We want to systematize these activities.

Fig 32 - The 80/20 Rule illustrates that inputs and outputs are not proportional

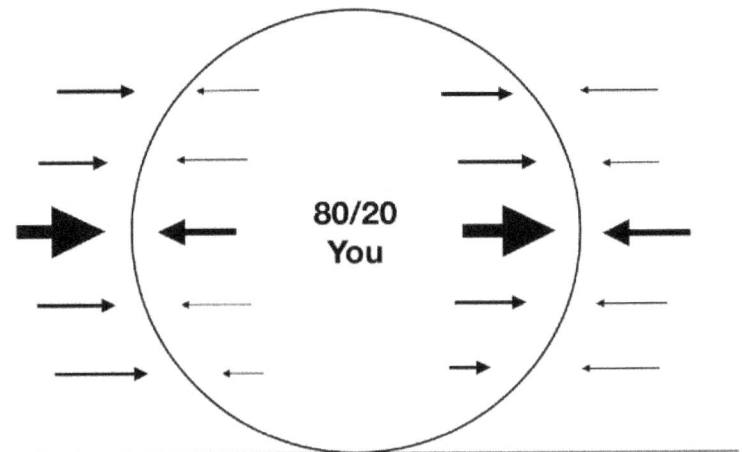

A few caveats to keep in mind about the 80/20 rule:

- it is not a law of physics
- the relationship is not always 80/20
- not all areas of life can be explained by the 80/20 rule
- 80/20 thinking is a tool *for prioritizing*; and finally,
- it can be easy to take it too far

From a Momentum Model point of view, the 80/20 rule helps us identify the big arrows from the little ones. It gives us a rough guess as to how much bigger some arrows can be. The quickest way to improve is to strengthen your biggest and strongest arrows. Then flip the 80/20 rule around and look at the negative behaviors holding you back. You always want to be moving forward, so reducing large negative forces is a great way to gain momentum (Fig 33).

Fig 33 - The 80/20 Rule can help us identify the relative strength (and importance) of the arrows in the Momentum Model

Back to Yogi Berra. He said baseball is 50% mental and 50% physical. But the 'mental half' drives 90% of the results. Seems obvious when you understand the 80/20 rule!

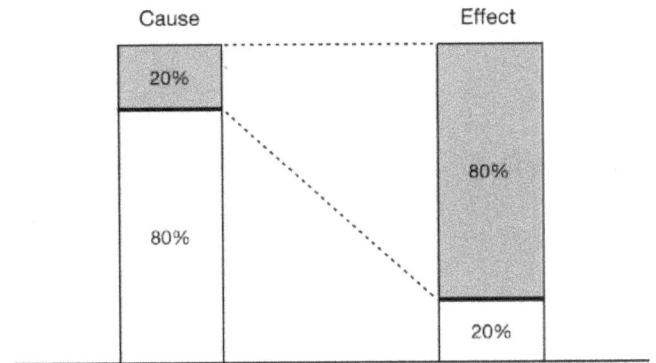

Build It In:

1. Are there practice activities that drive more improvement than others? What about study activities that drive most of your learning? Are there things you do that drive the majority of your negative results? Think about and write down a few areas of your life where the 80/20 rule probably holds true.

2. The 80/20 rule is particularly useful for prioritizing your time. What is the 20% of your day that drives the majority of your success?

3. Our lives are filled with "rest of 80%" activities. The trick is to keep these positive without putting extra effort into them. What are some of these activities?

4. What do you think: is running, like baseball, 90% mental?

Chapter 7: Causation

OTP #6: All behavior is caused. All causation is mental. We become what we think about most of the time.

We do the majority of our routines on auto-pilot. It's a survival mechanism. Thinking hard uses a lot of energy. Our ability to navigate the day without thinking hard allows us to keep a reserve of mental energy, which we draw from to exert willpower. This mental energy is so important that we've developed what I call the **Law of Conservation of Mental Energy**: if we *can* do something without thinking, we *will*.

When we learn a new skill or adopt a new routine, it takes a lot of willpower. It takes time before the behaviors become subconscious and we can both do them well and conserve our mental energy. We have to practice them enough to develop strong mental representations.

Our **mental representations** for an activity determine how efficiently and effectively we can do something. To do something well, we first need to have a well-defined understanding of what differentiates 'well done' from 'poorly done'. Experts have incredibly well-defined mental representations. Beginners typically do not.

Don't assume your training is optimal. At some point, you must revisit each area of your training to see if it can be improved. You are striving to do the most effective activities in the most efficient way (Fig 37). If you've never considered what you are doing, how can you be sure of either?

What do you spend your time thinking about? Great athletes maintain both their passion and concentration for years (Fig 38). This ensures they stay engaged, stay focused, and train purposefully. Athletes with lower passion or more distractions underperform as a result.

	Consideration		
	Actively	*Never*	*Previously*
Effect on Behavior — *Benefit*	Can create new effective behaviors	Potentially efficient	**Effective and efficient**
Effect on Behavior — *Drawback*	Highly inefficient	Potentially ineffective	Potentially ineffective (if circumstances have changed)

Fig 37 - Strive to have previously considered all of your important behaviors and habits

	Degree of Focus	
	Distraction	*Concentration*
Degree of Interest — *Passion*	Mistakes	Purposeful
Degree of Interest — *Disinterest*	Poor Behavior	Faking It

Fig 38 - "What We Think About Most of the Time" determines how we act most of the time

A few ideas to build better habits of thought:
- Make a public commitment: stating your goals in public takes advantage of our own psychology to make us more committed.
- Tomorrow's Key Three: Write down your top priorities for tomorrow, or this week. Share them with a teammate.
- Digital Cleanse: Go without your phone for a while. Delete an app that sucks away your time and attention. Practice spending that time thinking about your training or other core priorities.
- Tidy up: Clean and organize your room. Get rid of stuff that you don't need. Every decision to discard something is a decision that reinforces your priorities.

Build It In:

1. Systemize It: Say this to your coach and teammates: "Getting the most out of myself is a top priority. I'll do the best I can to achieve it." Even better: say it together.

2. Systemize It: Write down the different activities you do while training. Now choose an important one that you could do more efficiently (think 80/20!). Circle it. Commit yourself to work on that action specifically for the next couple weeks. If possible, recruit a teammate to do it with you.

3. On a scale of 1-5 (5 = high), how strong is your ability to concentrate?

4. Do you often find yourself making mistakes? What distractions can you remove to see if there is any improvement?

5. On a scale of 1-5, how passionate are you about training?

6. Do you often feel like you are faking it? What areas can you engage more to spark your passion?

7. Systemize It: A strong mental representation allows you to know exactly what you are trying to do. But it's not just in your mind. It's also in training your body to know how it's supposed to feel (muscle memory). Before your workout, identify what a high quality outcome should look and feel like. Focus on that standard while you train.

Chapter 8: Purpose

OTP #7: Optimal training is centered on clear, executable goals. We train to improve specific abilities. There are two types of goals: North Star goals (based on motivation) and Next Step goals (based on execution).

North Star goals are result-based and often exist in the future. There are numerous obstacles between us and our North Star goals, and the goals themselves can often seem a little crazy. Our society places a lot of emphasis on this type of goal. But North Star Goals are not the type of goals that will lead you to success. They can give you an idea of where you want to be, but they cannot dictate the path or tell you what to do now to make progress. For that, you need Next Step Goals.

Next Step goals are about the present. They are about following the best route. On top of being achievable today, they connect to the larger training program, require intense focus and concentration, and enhance our mental representations for specific activities. And they make up the core of purposeful practice, which is the most important of all the positive internal behaviors driving us forward (Fig 40).

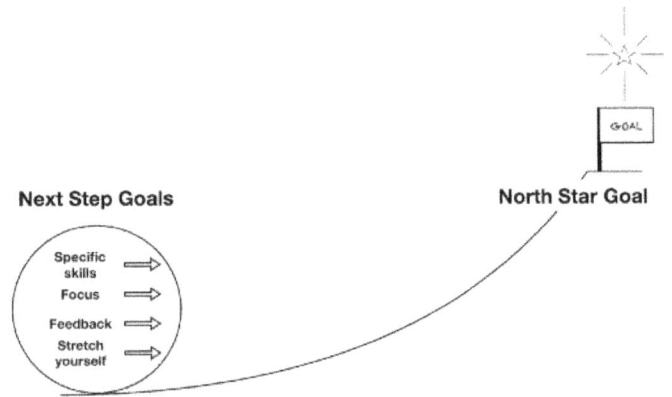

Fig 40 · Next Step goals push the ball forward today. North Star goals are where you hope to arrive.

Purposeful Practice is generally the best kind of practice available to you (though those with elite coaching can take it a bit higher). There are four main components of purposeful practice: Next Step goals, Focus, Immediate Feedback, and Getting Out of Your Comfort Zone. When you practice purposefully, you don't just do a workout. You use the workout to improve specific abilities. You focus intensely throughout, receive and act on constructive feedback, and physically or mentally push yourself out of your comfort zone.

When you focus on simply finishing the workout, you are doing **Naive Practice**. Just because you checked the box for the day doesn't mean you're improving. How you mentally approach your practice makes all the difference. Remember, it's about the feedback loop (Fig 41).

	Goals	Focus	Feedback	Comfort
Purposeful Practice	Well-defined, Specific	Intense, Sustained	Immediate, Specific	Outside comfort zone
Naive Practice	Undefined, General	Mild, Sporadic	Delayed, Generic	Inside comfort zone

Fig 41 - Purposeful Practice is a much more effective approach to training than Naive Practice

Dwight Eisenhower once said that plans are worthless, but planning is everything. Goals are the same. It's not about having big goals, it's about how you set goals: *Goals are worthless but goal setting is everything.*

Here are five strategies for setting North Star goals:

- Value check: Imagine *the lifestyle* it will take *to sustain* your goal. Does it excite you?
- Obstacles over Arrivals: try to identify as many obstacles as you can
- Backcast it: Imagine you already achieved it. How did you do it? Get specific.
- Do a pre-mortem: Imagine you failed. How many reasons can you come up with for why?
- Unfix your timeframe: Imagine you achieve it sooner vs later. What changes?

One last thing: whatever goal you create, *tell people about it*. You'll be much more likely to achieve it.

Build It In:

1. Write down your goals. Are they all motivational North Star goals? (It's ok if they are!) Just writing down our goals makes them more concrete, and boosts our commitment to them!

2. **Systemize It:** Think about yesterday's workout(s). On a scale of 1-5 (5 = high) grade yourself on the four factors of Purposeful Practice. Pick one area where you need to do better and make a plan to improve.

A. Clear Next Step goals:

B. Intense Focus:

C. Immediate Feedback:

D. Get Outside Comfort Zone:

3. **Systemize It:** Think about tomorrow's workout. What are one or two Next Step goals you can create to ensure you are maximizing the workout? Remember: a good Next Step goal improves a specific ability and requires intense focus. Run your goals by your coach and get his or her feedback.

4. Pick one of your North Star goals. How much thought have you put into the obstacles that could keep you from achieving it? Write down as many obstacles as you can think of. If you don't have a plan to overcome each of them, start planning!

Spotlight: Next Level 80/20

Question: What if we applied the 80/20 rule to itself? What is the top 20% of our top 20%? I call this the **Next Level 80/20**, and it looks like Figure 42 on the right. It tells us that nearly two thirds of our success is driven by just 4% of our efforts, and that two thirds of our daily efforts lead to just 4% of our success.

How about the next level after that? Well, we find that 1% of our activities account for 50% of our results (Fig 43).

(Wait, seriously?)

Yes!

But again, don't be concerned with numbers. This is a mental model. It's a way of thinking.

We train better when we assume that a small number of our activities generate the majority of our results, and we maximize our effort in those areas. Whether 1% of what we do drives 50% or 30% or 70% of our success, it doesn't change what we need to do. *We need to nail that 1%.*

Fig 42 - Next Level 80/20 takes our most important activities and applies the 80/20 Rule to them

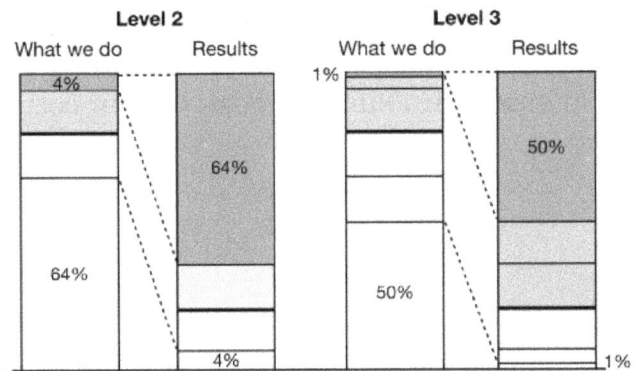

80/20 thinking doesn't stop at level 1. The goal of every athlete's training program is to create positive feedback loops, gain and sustain momentum, and make a leap. There is always one "Most Effective Activity" and it is enormously important.

Level 1 is to have an optimal training mindset. Approach every workout with the right mindset and attitudes. Engage in your training. Take responsibility. View everything through the lens of your effort and preparation. Build up your self-efficacy and develop strong mental habits.

Level 2 is to practice purposefully. Know what specific skills you are aiming to improve and what a high quality workout looks like. Set clear Next Step goals and stay hyper-focused on achieving them. Build better feedback into your training by asking better questions. Get out of your comfort zone, both physically and mentally.

Fig 43 - Next Level 80/20 tells us that 1% of our activities could lead to 50% of our success or failure

Level 3 is to do the work. Runners need to run hard. You're at least 50% of the way to success just by lacing up your shoes and hitting the roads hard day after day. This consistent effort is the core positive force driving your momentum forward.

For the rest of the 80%, keep it *positive*. The effects of these activities are smaller, but if enough of them are negative they will slow your momentum and keep you from making a leap. Use next level 80/20 thinking to figure out which of these are providing the least value and minimize how much time and energy you spend on them. We often have one person or one activity or one belief that holds us back more than all the rest. Find it and fix it.

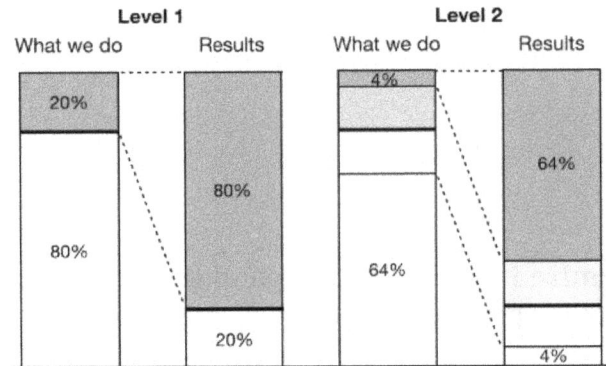

Build It In:

1. Do you agree that working hard every day is the top 1% activity that will lead to your success? What are you doing today to ensure you can put in maximum effort tomorrow?

2. Purposeful practice is essential to maximizing your efforts. Do you know what the purpose is for all of your workouts? Write down the purpose of your long run, your interval workouts, and your rest days. Do the same for stretching, weight training, and sleep. Now confirm with your coach.

3. An optimal training mindset ensures you are prioritizing the right activities and making good decisions. It involves engaging, taking responsibility, focusing on effort, and practicing purposefully. Do you feel you have an optimal training mindset? What is one area you can improve?

4. Next Level 80/20 says that 15 minutes of your day could result in 50% of your success. What might that 15 minutes be? Are you getting the most out of that 15 minutes today?

Chapter 9: Discipline

OTP #8: Certain behaviors, if practiced with consistent quality, ensure optimal training. Many athletes live undisciplined, unfocused lives that undermine their hard work. This is often related to what I call the **Discipline Illusion:** the idea that maintaining a disciplined lifestyle is restrictive and exhausting (Fig 44). The funny thing: *disciplined people don't feel this way!* They know they aren't sacrificing anything important and they haven't given up any freedom. They've simply focused on their priorities.

Even more important: disciplined people aren't working any harder than undisciplined people. In fact, they often use less willpower and make fewer decisions.

Two key factors that affect your discipline: your Lazy Default, and your Environment.

Your **Lazy Default** is what you do when you don't want to put energy into something. We do our lazy defaults because they are acceptable, routine, and easy. To improve your Lazy Default, make new rules for what you consider acceptable, make small changes to your routine, and simplify your activities by removing steps or extra friction.

	Decisions	Restrictions	Willpower
Discipline Illusion	Too many	Too many No freedom No fun	Too much Exhausting
Actual Experience	Fewer Well-considered	Few Low priority items	Less Conserved for practice

Fig 44 - The Discipline Illusion makes people think discipline is more exhausting than it is

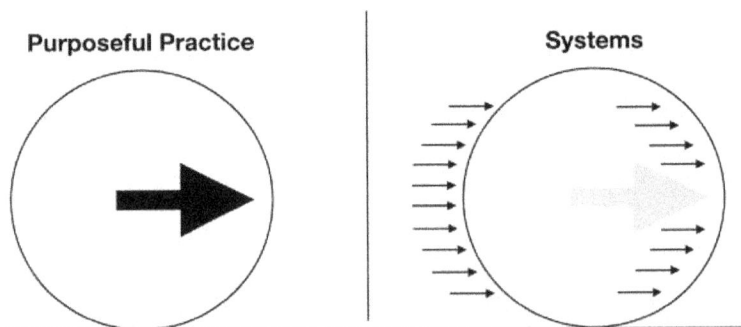

Your **Environment** contributes enormously to your discipline. This includes everything external: your team, school, work, family and friends, living space, and hobbies. Our environment is filled with **behavioral triggers** that influence what we choose to do, how well we do it, and how we feel about it afterwards. Fill your environment with high-quality triggers and you will improve your discipline (and your training, too).

What triggers should you focus on?
- Who you interact with (this is #1): interact with people who make you better, who help you to greater heights, who minimize negativity
- Create small reminders: a keychain, a message on the mirror, or a sticky note can all remind you to make the right decision.

Your goal is to create a **System**. Systems are anything you do regularly that sustain positive momentum. The best systems keep you going in the right direction with minimal effort. With systems, simplicity always wins. Create systems that either give you consistent positive boosts or that consistently avoid/remove what holds you back. A lifestyle based around purposeful practice and countless positive systems will lead you to make a leap (Fig 45).

Purposeful Practice

Systems

Fig 45 - Purposeful Practice creates a massive positive arrow. Systems create many small ones.

Build It In:

1. Most of our time is spent outside of training. Write down a list of all the activities you do. (You may need to write small!) Pick the one that can be improved the easiest with a simple system. Now do it!

2. What are your lazy default behaviors? What do you do when you don't feel like thinking? Write them down. Are there any that are currently harming your progress? Circle them. What rule or routine change would improve them?

3. Are you creating a disciplined environment for yourself? Do you have positive triggers reminding you to do what you need to do? Do you have negative aspects that create friction or hold you back? Pick a couple areas and write down what you can do to improve your environment.

4. **Systemize It:** Check in on the things you wrote down every month. Turn this check-in into a routine. Do it at the same time every week.

Do you see any improvement? If yes, pick a new one and do it again. If no, why not? Try a new approach. Test until you find what works for you.

Chapter 10: Mistakes

OTP #9: Making mistakes is an effective way to learn and improve. Mistakes can be essential, invigorating, and educational; that is, if you think about them the right way.

Mistakes are always mental. A mistake of commission occurs because of your direct action. A mistake of omission occurs when you fail to act and get a suboptimal result.

There are four main types of mistakes (Fig 46):

Laziness and Distraction are mistakes related to lack of attention and preparation, which leads to carelessness and disorganization. The solution starts with taking responsibility and adopting better systems.

Fear and Stress are more difficult to overcome. At a basic level it requires increasing self-efficacy, and improving your preparation and planning. It's not easy, but fear and stress can be overcome with experience and attention.

Ability to Correct

Type		Easier	Harder
	Omission	Laziness & Distraction	Fear & Stress
	Commission	Ignorance	Striving

Fig 46 - Mistakes typically fall into four main types based on why we make them and how correctable they are

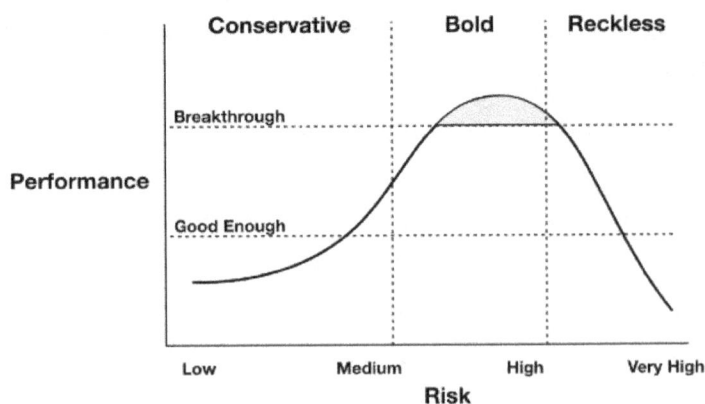

Ignorance is the simplest and most common reason we make mistakes; we don't know better. Ignorance is a part of life. You'll never know everything. But with targeted preparation and a willingness to put in the effort, you can eliminate the most obvious ignorant mistakes.

Striving mistakes happen when you try to do something for the first time, when you push your limits, aspire to do more and... don't get everything right. With striving mistakes, identifying the root cause is the challenge. It may seem obvious, but don't stop there; keep asking yourself questions until you figure out all the elements that went into you overdoing it. Striving mistakes are a risk every athlete must accept; but that's okay because *risk is tied to reward*.

Our ability to make a leap is tied to our ability to manage risk. There are three types of risk-taking: Conservative, Reckless, and Bold (Fig 47).

Conservative runners settle for good enough and rarely achieve breakthrough performances. Even worse: they don't learn about themselves and their true abilities.

Reckless runners always go for the breakthrough and often crash and burn. Exercising control is often their biggest problem. But their one advantage is they put themselves in position to do their best, albeit with great risk of failure!

Fig 47 - Achieving a breakthrough performance requires taking on risk; Bold runners plan to take on risk.

Bold runners prepare an aggressive plan in order to do their best. They minimize their downside while making a breakthrough possible. They don't guarantee their success—nothing can!—but they put themselves in the best position possible.

Mistakes in themselves are not shameful. How we handle them can be. Be bold, strive to continually improve, and when you make a mistake, course correct and learn from it.

Build It In:

1. Write down some recent mistakes. How would you categorize them? Do you see a pattern in the types of mistakes you are making?

2. How many of your recent mistakes are Striving mistakes? Write down a couple. What have you learned as a result of these striving mistakes?

3. If you have few striving mistakes, why do you think that is? Write down your thoughts and find ways to apply what you learn to your training.

4. Do you consider yourself to be generally conservative, bold, or reckless in your training? How about your racing?

5. If you are conservative, what scares you about taking on more risk?
If you are reckless, what scares you about being more conservative?
If you are bold, what is your strategy for not getting too conservative or too reckless?

6. What obvious areas for improvement or experimentation do you see? Write them down.

Chapter 11: Analysis

OTP #10: Racing times and personal records indicate progress at one point in time. You need to have a grasp on both where you are and how fast you are moving. That means having an idea of what is working and what needs improvement.

When looking at the big picture, it's best to focus on quality of execution. The same goes for analyzing specific races or practices. Remember, your leap will be based on the quality of your feedback loop, and that has to repeat over and over. Anything affecting that will hold you back, and results often hide the important takeaways.

Momentum check: Where you are isn't as important as where you're going and how fast you're moving. If you think tomorrow is looking better than today, you'll feel good. If your situation isn't what you want and you see no means to change it, you'll be dissatisfied. Every month, fill out the Momentum Model to consistently analyze your momentum.

Attribute better: Another strategy is to improve the way you attribute others' performances. *Fundamental Attribution Error* (what I also call the Talent Trap) leads us to attribute the actions of others to their internal qualities. We assume what they do is who they are, and if they are faster than us, it's a reflection of their talent (Fig 50).

When someone beats you, it means they were better than you on that day. Nothing more. There is nothing fixed about it that carries into the future, except that you may have some ground to make up to reach their current level. If they are training hard, you need to train harder. If they are preparing well, you need to prepare even better. Their performance is *also just an indication of their progress at one point in time*, so there's nothing stopping them from increasing the gap as well.

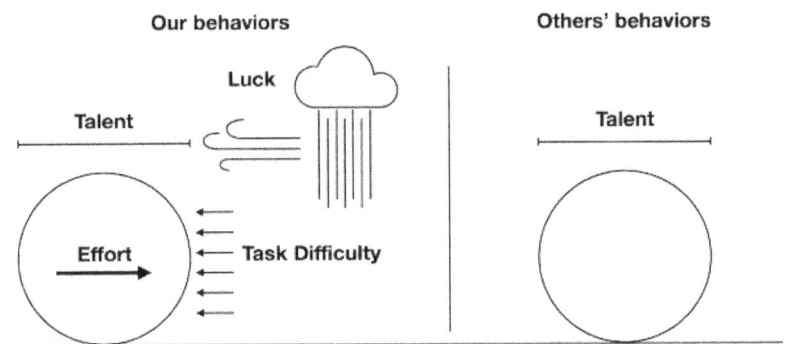

Fig 50 · Fundamental Attribution Error and Talent Trap associate all performance with talent, and neglect other key factors

Fix your feedback: Not all feedback is positive. You need critical feedback to point out where you can get better. Rule number one of communication: most people aren't good at it, so try not to judge the specific words. Separate the message from how it makes you feel and try to look at it from their perspective. Just because you don't like it doesn't mean it's unfair.

For all other criticism, convert it to effort-based terms ("gawdawful" = poorly executed). Effort is the one factor we can control. It doesn't make sense to analyze our results against any other factor. The focus should be on how you can prepare for and work your way through challenging situations in the future.

Performances are just a reflection of a point in time (Fig 51). So is your analysis. Create systems to keep it up-to-date.

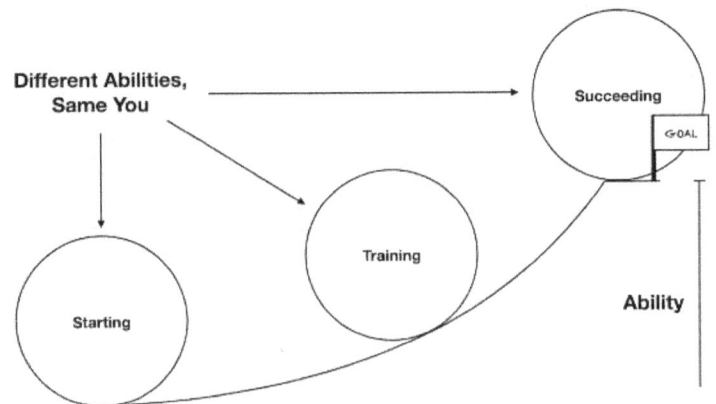

Fig 51 · Your performance is just an indication of your ability at a specific point in time

Build It In:

1. Who do you want to be? Who are you now? How big is that gap?

2. Think of someone you aspire to be like. What qualities led to their success? Write those qualities down.

3. You can't wait for success to build the habits that will sustain it. Does your lifestyle today align to the qualities you listed above?

How can you analyze these qualities to keep yourself on track?

4. What does the quote, "Respect your position while preparing for your promotion" mean to you?

5. **Understand It:** How do you spend your time? To find out, create a daily activity log. Track your time in 15 minute increments (I find this to be an 80/20 level of granularity). Write down what you did and also how you felt. Do this for a couple weeks and look for patterns.

6. **Systemize It:** When you receive criticism, find a way to convert it into effort-based terms. Do this over and over until it becomes a system. It will help your training immensely!

Chapter 12: Perseverance

OTP #11: Optimal performances and realizing your potential are results of painstaking preparation and hard work. Your goal should be to realize your potential. To run as fast as your physical and mental talents will permit. Every other goal is a milestone on that journey.

In order to realize your potential, you first need to improve on a shorter time frame. You need to run your best today, tomorrow, and every day after that. Build momentum today, sustain momentum tomorrow.

Build momentum today (Think Big): Prioritize improving your largest, most powerful internal forces. You need to get the big things right, because it's the big things that most determine our momentum and progress. A small change to a big force often has a larger effect than a big change to a small force. Get engaged. Set better Next Step goals. Improve your environment.

Removing large negative forces is essential, or at minimum reducing them. Remember: no matter how big a problem feels, there is always a way to improve it. Dig in and find it (Fig 52).

Sustain momentum tomorrow (Think Small, Think All): It is hard work to create new systems, but you need lots of them to sustain your momentum. Keep making small improvements to both your mindset and your physical environment. Your future effort will build on your current effort, so don't try to do it all now. With each boost in momentum you should feel a little more committed. A little more engaged. A little more motivated. Use those feelings to help make the next small change. And repeat, and repeat, and repeat (Fig 53).

Consistency is key. Don't worry about perfection, just improvement. The improvement will compound on itself. One small change maintained over time can lead to a small leap. *Many small changes maintained over time can lead to a big leap.* You won't see the changes immediately. But given enough time, they will make a difference.

The biggest benefit of consistently working on these small forces is the sense of commitment and engagement you create. The more you succeed, the more you define yourself as someone in control of your life and your performances. The more you feel this way, the easier it is to keep doing the necessary work.

To be the best, you can't just out-work your competition. *You need to out-think and out-live your competition.* Believe in yourself and your abilities. Commit to the long haul. Create a positive feedback loop filled with positive internal and external forces. And then be patient and put in the work. You *will* make the leap.

Short term

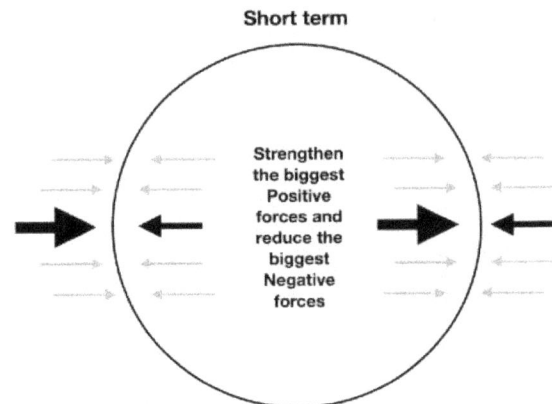

Fig 52 - Short term: identify and improve all of the biggest forces affecting your performance

Longer term

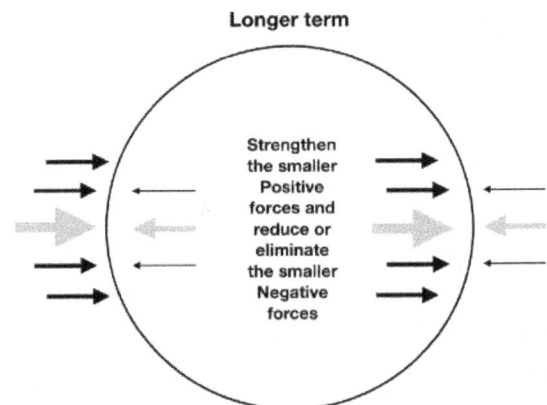

Fig 53 - Long term: focus on improving all of the small arrows (Think Small, Think All)

Build It In:

1. List three major negative forces in your life. What can you do today to chip away at those negative forces? Make a plan and get going.

2. **Systemize it:** Every week, come up with at least one small negative force you'd like to remove and devote the week to removing it. Build the change into your systems so you don't have to spend time thinking about it!

What small change do you want to work on this week? What are you going to do?

3. How's your support network? Do you have a mentor? If so, make sure you set up a schedule for talking with them. If not, who would be an ideal mentor? Ask them if they would be willing to give you advice.

4. Most people fail not because something stops them, but because they stop themselves. How committed are you to achieving your potential? Write it down and tell someone!

About Bryan Green

Bryan Green is the co-founder of Go Be More apparel, where he also co-hosts the Go Be More Podcast. He lives in Sendai, Japan with his wife and two daughters. Prior to moving to Japan he used the same mindset in this book to excel in his career at Apple and to learn Japanese and Italian as an adult.

He competed at UCLA from 1997 to 2002, and was a two-time individual qualifier to the NCAA Cross Country Championships in 2000 and 2001.

HS bests (3rd fastest time*)
800m: 1:59 (2:00)
1600m: 4:23 (4:26)
3200m: 9:22 (9:29)
XC (3mi): 15:17 (15:35)

Collegiate bests
1500m: 3:50.1 (3:52)
5000m: 14:19 (14:22)
10000m: 29:25 (29:40)
XC (8k): 23:57 (24:11)

* My teammate Scott Abbott used to argue that one's 3rd fastest time is a more accurate reflection of their actual ability. I agree.

maketheleapbook@gmail.com
maketheleapbook.com
@maketheleapbook
gobemore.co

Get my newsletter!

Sign up at maketheleapbook.com/newsletter.

www.ingramcontent.com/pod-product-compliance
Lightning Source LLC
Chambersburg PA
CBHW080939040426
42443CB00015B/3475